The Proven Self Inside You

Merris Chacko

BookLeaf Publishing

India | USA | UK

Made with ❤ on the BookLeaf Publishing Platform
www.bookleafpub.in
www.bookleafpub.com

Dedication

To the "You Inside You"—the quiet, constant force that chose the challenge and saw it through. May this collection serve as proof that the most worthy words are found not in speed, but in the patience to go that extra mile.

Preface

This book offers no guide, no grand analysis, and no roadmap to self-awareness. Instead, it is a simple invitation: a collection of quiet thoughts best paired with the steam of a cup of tea.

When the last sip is taken, the hope is you feel refreshed. These poems are designed not to correct, but to initiate a self-check—an honest moment of observation between the "you inside you" and the rest of the world.

In a life demanding constant noise, may these pages bring you to that brief, focused center, reminding you that your proven self is always worth the pause.

Acknowledgements

First, to the **You Inside You**: thank you for insisting on the truth, choosing that **extra mile**, and proving your worth with every line. This journey was undertaken to honor you.

To my family and friends—you are the silent, steady background against the world's noise. Thank you for giving me the space and grace to be absent while these poems found their voice.

And finally, to the reader, for pausing your busy life to share this quiet focus. Thank you for granting these words the most important gift of all: your time.

1. I, Me, and Myself

I, me, and myself.
If they compete, who will be the winner?
If I win, I will be happy.
If me wins, I will be happy.
The truth is simple: when I focus on I, me, and myself —
everything else follows.

I told me to be profound
Me told myself to be skilled
I told me to ace it in everything
Me told myself to be anything

I told me to be kind
Me told myself to be bold
I told me to be empathetic
Me told myself to be magnetic

I told me to shine with grace
Me told myself to run the race
I told me to rise, never fall
Me told myself I can have it all

When I, me and myself speaks to each other
They may say they don't know each other

When I, me and myself is one
None can fathom the oneness begun

2. The Lord of crystal

To the soul that bears the weight,
Be the Snowflake at the gate;
A softness settling, light and low,
To cool the fever, melt the woe.

To the hands that reach in need,
Be the Salt, the vital seed;
The lasting worth, the honest grace,
A stable strength within that space.

And when you look upon your core,
Be the diamond, and nothing more;
Unbreakable, with edges keen,
The brightest strength that you have seen.

3. The Field That Matters

The Playing Field matters,
It shapes the will, it scatters
The crowd, defining every stride,
And where our true ambition hides.

Are you running a race bound to the dirt of a familiar
place?
Where the finish line is clear, And victory is earned year
by year?
Or are you in a Mission to Space, Searching for a
boundary-less place?
A different gravity to fight, Where failure is just altered
light?

Play right, play to win the race,
Use every skill, maintain your pace;
The rules are known, the path is set,
A common triumph you will get.

Fail to win the space,
That cosmic, risk-filled, unknown chase;
For in that grand, unmeasured field,
The greatest, truest self is revealed.

4. One day at a time

Countless numbers are all around,
The chase is well-surrounded.
What matters is just one day at a time,
Stay where it all started, at the prime.

Start the day and start the way,
Believe in full stops at the bay.
Everything has an end,
There is no endlessness in the amendment.

There is a time for everything,
There is a composure for anything.
Make a profound choice of your own,
Dodge the things that keep you from the ground.

Twice is unfathomable, so is thrice
Winning is applauded, so is a fall in price.
The beauty of day one is overly refined,
As compared to the last day when it is defined.

Time is bound to teach the value in you,
Go to day one with the belief of winning.
What the rule is: one day at a time,
Measured, scaled, and weighted.

5. Time Tailored

The clock's nature is to move with the sun,
Its minutes are measured one by one.
But you are not part of that vast machine,
Your day's design is a landscape yet unseen.

The thread of time is given, strong and true,
A universal fabric, folded and saved.
But the needle's path, the cut, the careful fold,
Is yours to master, brave and bold.
It's not about the forty hours that must be spent,
But where the focus is truly sent.
Don't let the moment make its choice,
Define the shape you wish your day to take.

Dismiss the rush and call of the calendar,
And ask the mirror: "What is essential to me?"
The two-hour building what is great,
The fifteen-minute pause you set apart.
The hour devoted to climb the ladder,
To reach the peak or to reach the valley.

So take your shears to reject the fear,
And stitch the border for the battle.
For every second wasted leaves a mark,

And every moment tailored conquers the fear.

Live not in borrowed time, nor time that's vast,
But in the perfect measure made to last.
Measured, scaled, and weighted—by your hand,
A finished garment that you understand.

6. 6. Sunshine and Moonshine

Remember this: everything that shines is full—
Some bright, some mild, some dull.
The voice that fades your inner light is the true enemy,
Not a lack of brilliance in you.
Put yourself in a place where you can shine,
For you can't decide *how* to shine or *not* to shine.

A line drawn can go a long way, but can never return.
So radiate like a beam that goes far and never looks back.
Time is yours until you see the break of day;
Don't fear the times you can't see the sun.
Be glad that throughout your life, you have seen enough
sunshine.

Focus until you can see the moonlight,
And remember, always take a good night's rest.
The moon has dimmed its light so you may rest;
So too, dim your light for others to shine bright.
Let the world know that others cannot define you,
When you know when to be summer and when to be
winter.

7. 7. A Canvas of Worth

In the mirror's glass, a new day takes its hold,
No flawless face the legends have been sold.
But here I stand, beneath the morning's bright appeal,
A deeper truth, a vibrant strength to feel.

The self-proven spirit, a soft, resilient gleam,
Reflected in the shimmer of a waking dream.
With brush in hand, no mask do I compose,
But highlight where the authentic spirit glows.

A subtle sweep of eyeshadow, a neutral, earthy hue,
To frame the gaze that knows exactly what is true.
A touch of blush upon the cheeks, a flush of inner fire,
Kindled not by others' praise, but my own strong desire.

The lip, perhaps, a bold, unapologetic red,
A quiet sign of every word I've finally said.
This makeup, then, a choice, a joyful, bright array,
A celebration of the power that is mine today.

And on the fingertip, a small and polished shield,
A canvas where my silent vows are now revealed.
The nail paint dries, a solid, steadfast coat,
A shade of courage, the quietest anecdote.

9

For every chip and crack, a battle understood,
The journey traveled to where I always stood.
This brilliant gleam of polish, a deep and vibrant dye,
Is the external promise of my ingrained self-worth, held
high.

No need to seek approval in another's glance, My own
reflection offers me the only honest chance. The beauty I
apply is simply meant to trace The quiet, settled wisdom
of a self-accepted grace.

8. The Untrainable Track

The whistle blows, a wild and piercing cry,
The train that cannot be trained, it rushes by.
It shakes the earth, a massive iron will,
Rebelling 'gainst the straightness of the hill.

The train thought it's ready to be trained,
Imagine the machine, its stubbornness restrained.
It slowed its wheels, it tried to run the line,
But destiny had drawn another sign.

For freedom is a thunder in its steam,
A force that shatters every ordered dream.
It pulls and bucks against the coupling chain,
Determined to feel wildness in the rain.

If the mind must change, then hear the simple claim:
Train the brain if you don't want to train
The frantic engine, let the inner self be free,
Let thought become the calming constancy.

Refine the mind, the engine of the soul,
To guide the great momentum to its goal.
And whisper to the steel, a gentle, guiding art,
Train the train not to be harsh of heart.

For power untamed is merely wasteful flight,
But power with compassion finds the light.
Let the fierce, roaring iron learn to glide,
With disciplined strength and peace held deep inside.

9. Not Everyone's Friend

Life isn't about a marathon of friends,
Nor about being in the good books of others.
It isn't about sharing with the countless,
Or chasing the likes and thumbs-up of strangers.

Courageous are the ones disliked —
They don't bother to be friend or frenemy.
Courageous are the ones who face hate —
They don't seek who claps or who turns away.
Courageous like a one-man army —
They march on, unfazed by who follows.

The road is wide, but not for everyone to join.
Only the ones you choose
Should walk beside you in it.

10. Learn to Dismiss

Dismiss the chaotic world so there is a world you know,
The time you know how it ticks, The surrounds that
know you, The road that remembers you,
The wall that realized it's you who has walked in.
Be where you want to belong, not where you belong.

The value of the sense, the feeling of belonging,
Happens when you're there your whole life.
Stay in a new place for over a decade, you will feel you
belong there,
To really know it's your place, whether to ponder it, You
know it when you look within.
Do you feel the road knows you? Do you feel the walls
understood you?
Do you think so, is it where you belong?
Stay where you want to be, not where you belong.

11. 11. The Coordinates of Choice

Dismiss the noise, and the frantic sweep
A chosen world remains, where all truths are known
The clock's heart is steady; you know how its time ticks true,
The surrounds are observant, they look out and know you.
The road has a memory, it registers your passing tread,
And the wall seems to straighten, realizing it's you who has fled

And returned.

Be where you want to belong, not where you merely reside.

12. The Decade's Root

The value of belonging is not given but earned,
A quiet, slow harvest for which the soul has yearned.
It's built over decades, a whole life given to ground,
For in a new place, after ten years, that feeling is found.
To know if it's truly your spot, your permanent hold,
You don't need a map or a story to be told;
 You know it for certain when you search within.

Ask the silence: Does the asphalt know where your
journey has been?
Do the walls, stiff and sturdy, understand the person you
are?
If the answer is yes, then you've traveled beyond far.

Stay where you want to be, not where you are told to
belong.
This chosen connection is where you are always strong.

13. The Color You Must Defend

A blue fish in a glass bowl, serene and fine,
It holds its silent color, a perfect, chosen line.
The self in you has colors, a deep and hue,
A voice that speaks in beauty, showing what is true.

It calls when you are standing at the edge of all selection,
whispering to your spirit:
You like what you like—hold its direction.
The color you love will follow, reflected everywhere,
So choose that vibrant pigment, and keep it near, keep it
rare.

For when you do the thing you love, your inner light is
showing,
It proves you are alive, authentically glowing.
But to deny that yearning, to choose a path untrue,
 Is to end in a wrong color—a fading shade for you,

And for the gentle fish that swam its way to find you.
Be fiercely selective; paint the world that should bind
you.
Fill the things you long to be with hues you can defend,
Your spirit's true bright color, right up until the end.

14. Check for the Errors in You

Before you check the world for faults,
Run a scan within your own lines —
See where your logic loops in doubt,
And where your truth still aligns.

Pause the rush to mark "passed" or "failed,"
Some tests are meant to stay unknown;
You debug courage, one break at a time,
In scripts life never clearly shown.

Check for the errors in you —
Not to judge, but to renew;
Each flaw, a hint the code can grow,
Each warning, a light breaking through.

Refactor your heart with patience,
Comment your scars with grace;
You are still in deployment,
Yet stable in His embrace.

So before you sign off your day,

Run one last test, quiet and true —
Forgive the version you once were,
And check for the errors in you

15. The Trees Know Better

Look at the trees and plants —
they grow from what they have.
No envy in their branches,
no shame in their shade.

No two trees compare their fruits,
nor whisper who is more mighty.
The mango doesn't envy the neem,
the rose never doubts the lily.

They rise in silence,
rooted in what's theirs.
They bloom in their season,
unrushed, unbothered, aware.

If only we too could learn —
to grow from what we have,
and stop measuring our light by another's sun.

16. The Signature of Self

The pen is not equivalent to keyboards click,
And that sharp difference is the soul I now must pick.
The keyboard hums with speed, a thousand drafts in flight,
But the ink I lay is mine, in the sun and in the night.
When I hold the stylus, the world shrinks to the page,
It's a deliberate journey, turning a new age.
No backspace button cheers me, no easy, quick *undo*,
Just the courage of commitment in every line I push through.
The uniform font of the machine, all letters are the same,
It prints the common language of fortune, sport, and fame.
But my handwriting—bent, imperfect, slow, and full of care
 It is the only proof that I was truly, deeply there.

Let others race the algorithm, let them chase the fleeting trend,
 My self-worth is anchored where the flowing waters bend.
 It's in the messy margin, the blot, the *personal* flaw,
It's the un-digitized truth of the thought that I withdraw.
So let the digital bells chime, let the screens glow bright

and wide,
I am the author of my own worth, with nothing left to
hide.
The pen is a vessel of spirit, a signature of self,
A priceless, original tool, not meant for a cold shelf.

17. The Unwritten

When the remedy is unknown, and the cure is not known,
Let the mind decree a quiet, and build its inner throne.
For every searching science, and every fevered plea,
There is a greater current flowing, wild and utterly free.

Have the mind to think it's okay—a radical, soft grace,
To find the center steady, in this unsettling space.
Let panic be a shadow, let worry lose its sting,
And trust the soul's deep measure, for the strength that peace can bring.

The answer is not written on any earthly chart;
It is woven in the patience that settles in the heart.
The cure, perhaps, is learning how to breathe and stand this test,
And finding wholeness now, with the knowing of the rest.

18. The Wasted Hour

The hands creep round the clock face slow,
While phantom worries come and go.
No rest is earned, no task is done,
Just chasing thoughts beneath the moon.
These vacant hours—they are not worth
The heavy price they claim on earth.
I trade the dark for morning's light,
Sleepless nights are not worth the fight.

The rising sun finds nothing new,
No mountain scaled, no promise true.
The chance to build, to dream, to mend,
Was lost before the hour's end.
And all that's left is bitter dread,
For time that's gone and words travelled.
The clock forgives no moment brief;
 It only deepens my belief:
A minute spent in thoughtful haste, Is better than a
lifetime's waste.

19. 19. The Proven Self Rests

The proven self has battles fought and won,
 Its worth established when the light is done.
 I know the strength within, the road I've walked, So
why, in shadows, should my mind be mocked?

These hollow hours, where worries twist and turn,
 Are a poor investment for the fires that burn.
 This restless night is an unworthy cost— My proven
energy is better saved than lost.

20. 20 . The Inner Knowing

The you inside you holds a steady light,
It doesn't need the volume to prove its might.
It knows the bedrock truth, firm and profound,
That you are worthy, even without a sound.

If you know this deep truth, then let it stand;
No mirror, fear, or future can demand
A better reason to be strong and free—
The proof of worth resides eternally in thee.

21. Go That Extra Mile

The road you travel stretches past the sign,
Where others pause and call the finish line.
But the proven you inside has learned to know The
truest harvest is where the hardest seeds grow.

It's in the quiet depth of one more stride,
The final, unseen choice where failures hide;
That extra mile—unwatched, un-applauded, free— Is the
sacred ground of your supremacy.

Here, every nerve affirms the strength you claim,
Refining effort to an inner flame.
For only past the point of simple "done," Is the
exceptional, true self completely won.